DR. CHARLES DREW

MEDICAL PIONEER

"Dream high enough
and work hard enough,
and we'll all get
to where we want to go."
⌐ Dr. Charles Drew ⌐

BY SUSAN WHITEHURST

The Child's World®
childsworld.com

Published by The Child's World®
1980 Lookout Drive • Mankato, MN 56003-1705
800-599-READ • www.childsworld.com

PHOTOS

Cover and page 4: Alfred Eisenstaedt/The LIFE Picture Collection via Getty Images
Interior: Afro American Newspapers/Gado/Archive Photos via Getty Images:
23; Courtesy of the Moorland-Spingarn Research Center: 5, 8, 9, 10, 11, 12, 13, 14,
15, 16, 18, 20, 21, 24, 25, 26, 28, 29, 31; Everett Collection/Newscom: 17; Everett
Collection/Shutterstock.com: 19; Harris & Ewing/Library of Congress, Prints and
Photographs Division: 7; J.W. Moulton and John S. Moulton/Library of Congress,
Prints and Photographs Division: 6; U.S. National Library of Medicine: 22

LIBRARY OF CONGRESS CATALOGING-IN-PUBLICATION DATA
ISBN 9781503854451 (Reinforced Library Binding)
ISBN 9781503854918 (Portable Document Format)
ISBN 9781503855298 (Online Multi-user eBook)
LCCN: 2021930464

Printed in the United States of America

Cover and page 4 caption:
Dr. Charles Drew in 1946.

CONTENTS

4

Chapter One

UP FROM FOGGY BOTTOM

During the time of slavery, large numbers of free African Americans moved to Washington, DC. It was the only southern city where they were able to create their own society. By 1900, the African Americans there had established a successful community with its own schools, businesses, churches, and clubs.

This was the world into which Charles Richard Drew was born on June 3, 1904. He was born in his grandmother's three-story home on E Street in Foggy Bottom, Washington, DC. Six years later, the family moved to another home down the block.

Foggy Bottom was a great place to live. The Drew children could fish and swim in the river, play in the parks, and visit the museums and monuments in the capital city.

Charles Drew around 1924 as a college student

Foggy Bottom was filled with people from many different backgrounds, including African, Irish, French, and Italian Americans. Washington was **segregated**, however. Although Black and white children played ball together in Foggy Bottom's vacant lots, they still had to attend separate schools and use separate swimming pools.

Charlie's own background was as varied as his neighborhood. His grandparents and great-grandparents were Native American, Scottish, English, and African. His rich heritage contributed to Charlie's red hair, light skin, and freckles.

Charlie's father, Richard, was a carpet layer at the Moses Furniture Company. He was a big, friendly man who played the piano and guitar. Charlie's mother, Nora, was a graduate of Howard University and a schoolteacher. After Charlie was born, Nora gave up teaching to stay home and raise the children.

> Foggy Bottom got its name because mist from the nearby Potomac River would often blanket the low-lying neighborhood with fog.

A crowd of Black students on the lawn of Howard University in 1867.

6

The five Drew children—Charlie, Elsie, Nora, Joseph, and Eva—grew up in a home filled with books and music. They all had chores to do, such as washing dishes, setting the table, cleaning house, and taking care of their clothes. Their parents encouraged them to do well in school and to have jobs. Charlie's mother often reminded the children that they had to work and study hard. "Don't you ever forget," she would tell them, "that you were cared for and educated by your father, who worked on his knees."

Charlie started working when he was 12 years old. He sold newspapers on the street corners. Charlie was very good at selling newspapers. As his business grew, he asked his brother Joe to help him sell copies of the *Washington Times* and the *Herald*.

A newsboy in Washington, DC holding the *Washington Times* in 1915.

When the business grew too big for two boys, Charlie hired six others to sell the papers. They would go downtown every afternoon and sell the papers outside the big office buildings. Some days they would sell 2,000 papers.

Charlie was already showing signs of his determination and his skills as a manager and an organizer. As a teenager, he worked at construction sites. One summer he worked in a glass-making factory. Inside the factory, the temperature often reached more than 100 degrees.

The Drew family regularly attended the Nineteenth Street Baptist Church. Both Charlie and his dad sang in the choir. Charlie was deeply **influenced** by the Reverend Walter Brooks. Reverend Brooks often told the people at his church that they should serve the community. Charlie listened to Reverend Brooks and remembered his words. One day, Charlie vowed, he would dedicate his life to serving others.

Charles Drew (in tie) with his brother and sisters in 1914.

At Dunbar High School, Charlie (back row, third from right) played a sport each season.

When Charlie was a teenager, Washington, DC had the best high school in the country for African Americans. Dunbar High School was the only free school for Black students that offered college-preparatory classes. It was named after Paul Laurence Dunbar, a famous African American poet. Dunbar High School offered classes in Greek, Latin, chemistry, and biology.

Charlie was a good student and a top athlete. He loved to play sports. Each season, he played a different sport. In the fall, he played football. In the winter, it was basketball. He kept busy in the spring with track and baseball, and in the summer he swam.

Chapter Two

SPRINTING THROUGH LIFE

Before Charlie finished high school, tragedy struck his home. His sister Elsie died of **tuberculosis** in 1920. Her long illness and death affected Charlie deeply. He began to think of studying medicine and becoming a doctor. But at that time, Black doctors were not welcomed in the medical community. Most medical schools accepted only one or two Black students a year. There were only two medical schools in the United States that welcomed large numbers of Black students. But even when African Americans became doctors, many hospitals wouldn't hire them.

Charlie (top row, far left) and the Dunbar High School basketball team in 1921.

The Drew family left Foggy Bottom after Elsie died. They moved a few miles away to a two-story house in Arlington, Virginia. But Charlie continued to go to Dunbar. He knew it was the best high school for Black students who wanted to go to college.

Charlie graduated from Dunbar High School in 1922. His classmates thought very highly of him. In fact, they voted him the best athlete, the most popular student, and the student who had done the most for the school.

Charlie as a student at Amherst College in 1925.

Amherst College in Massachusetts gave Charlie a partial **scholarship**. In the 1920s, Amherst was a small men's college, and most of the students were white. There were only a few Black students, but that didn't stop Charlie. He starred on both the football team and the track team. He was especially valued for his "second effort"—long after he could have given up, he could gain another yard or score another point.

Charlie's fame on the sports field made many of the white players jealous. This was Charlie's first daily experience with **racial** hatred and slurs. After one big game, the football team went out to dinner at a hotel. The hotel asked Charlie and the other Black team members to eat somewhere else. Insults like this made Charlie so mad that his face would turn red, earning him the nickname "Big Red." Charlie made a decision about his anger that would influence the rest of his life. He decided to fight the racial attacks by being the very best person he could be. Charlie said, "I won't use violence against racial attacks. Our race can progress by showing our talents." And that's just what he did.

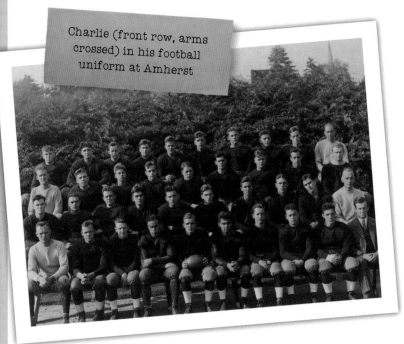

Charlie (front row, arms crossed) in his football uniform at Amherst

Amherst College knew Charlie was smart. They expected more from him than sports awards. So when his grades started to slip, he was called in to see the **dean**. The dean asked Charlie which was more important to him, his studies or sports. Charlie was certainly good enough to become a professional athlete. "But remember, Mr. Drew," the dean told him, "Negro athletes are a dime a dozen."

Charlie knew he wanted to become a doctor. He took the dean's warning seriously. He continued to play sports, but he doubled his efforts in class. His grades improved immediately. During one of Amherst's football games, Charlie was badly injured. In the last seconds of the game, he grabbed the ball and ran for a touchdown. He was tackled at the goal line, but he stretched out his arm as he was going down, and scored. Touchdown! But before Charlie could get up, another player stomped on his leg with the cleats of his football shoe. In the early 1900s, football players wore little padding. The cleats went right into Charlie's thigh.

Charlie had to be rushed to the hospital to save his leg. But sometimes accidents can turn into opportunities. Charlie's doctor invited him to come along as he visited other patients in the hospital. One patient Charlie met had almost died during surgery because the hospital's supply of blood was low. There had been barely enough blood to give him a life-saving **transfusion**.

Charles Drew's graduation photograph from 1926.

Charlie's leg healed, but the accident left him with a walnut-sized hole in his leg—and the beginnings of his career as a doctor. "I got banged up in football and wanted to know how the body works," Charlie said years later.

After he graduated from Amherst with honors in 1926, Charlie knew he wanted to go to medical school. He didn't have enough money, however, so he returned home and took a job at Morgan State College in Baltimore, Maryland. He was Morgan's athletic director and also taught biology and chemistry, earning $1,500 a year.

Two years later, Charlie had saved enough money for medical school. But at that time, most medical schools in the United States still accepted only one or two Black students a year. Charlie applied to Howard University in Washington, DC. and to Harvard University in Boston. Howard turned him down because he hadn't taken enough English classes at Amherst. Harvard said he could come, but that he'd have to wait a year. Charlie didn't want to wait that long.

Howard University was founded in 1867. It was named after General Oliver Otis Howard, a Civil War hero. Just five years after opening, the university had already educated more than 150,000 formerly enslaved people.

Charlie was very disappointed that he wasn't accepted to Howard. He could have saved money by living with his parents, because Howard was close to their home. But the rejection only made Charlie more determined. He vowed that one day he would return to Howard University.

In the meantime, Charlie needed to find another medical school. McGill University in Montreal, Canada, accepted him because he was talented, smart, and a hard worker. McGill's professors thought Charlie would be a fine doctor. He proved them right. In 1933, he graduated at the top of his class as a doctor of medicine and a master of surgery.

One of Drew's professors at McGill changed his life forever. Dr. John Beattie was visiting from England. He saw Drew's eagerness to learn and invited him to go to the hospital to watch the experiments Dr. Beattie was doing with blood.

Far into the night, Drew and Beattie talked about blood. They discussed how to store it and how to use it safely. Transfusions were being performed and saving lives, but there were still problems with this technique.

Drew (center) and other doctors at the Montreal General Hospital in 1935.

Human beings have four major blood types: A, B, AB, and O. For a transfusion to be successful, the blood must come from someone with the same blood type. If a doctor gives a patient the wrong blood, the patient could die.

Drew (right) with his father and brother

There were also challenges when it came to storing the blood. Blood starts to break down after 24 hours. It can be refrigerated for just one week. When a doctor needed a blood transfusion for a patient, a donor with the same blood type had to be found right away. Once, Drew had to donate his own blood for a patient who was already on the operating table. Drew was the only person there with the patient's blood type.

Drew stayed in Montreal for two more years to complete his residency, the training period in which new doctors work in a hospital. Months after Canada **certified** Drew as a surgical specialist, his father died suddenly.

Drew went home to be close to his family and again applied to Howard University, this time as a teacher. Howard hired him as a teacher for $150 a month and as a surgeon at Freedmen's Hospital, a facility run by the university. Freedmen's Hospital was founded in 1862 to treat the large numbers of Black residents moving to Washington, DC, during and after the Civil War (1861–1865). At the time, formerly enslaved people were called "freed men." The hospital later became the teaching hospital for the teachers and students of Howard University.

Three years later, in 1938, Drew decided to continue his surgical studies. He was awarded a **fellowship** to Columbia University Medical School in New York City.

Drew at a Howard University lab in 1940.

While at Columbia-Presbyterian, Drew was assigned to Dr. John Scudder. Dr. Scudder was leading a research team to study blood chemistry and transfusions. In 1939, Columbia-Presbyterian opened a blood bank and named Drew as its director.

It was during this time that Drew met Minnie Lenore Robbins. While Traveling to Alabama, he stopped in Atlanta, Georgia, to have dinner with an old friend. The friend introduced Drew to Minnie, a 28-year-old home economics teacher at Spelman College. Minnie often went by "Lenore."

Minnie Lenore Robbins attended Spelman College in Atlanta, Georgia. Founded in 1881, it was the first college for Black women in the United States.

"The moment I saw him, I knew he was a man to be reckoned with—and the man for me," said Lenore. "Three nights later, on his way back north, he roused the matron of our dormitory at one o'clock in the morning and insisted that she wake me. I went down to meet Dr. Drew on the moonlit campus. He proposed to me then and there. Six months later, we married and began our life together in New York City."

Chapter Three

NOTHING'S IMPOSSIBLE

Lenore was astonished to learn that her new husband had
two difficult jobs: one as an operating surgeon at Columbia-
Presbyterian Medical Center, and the other as a member of
Dr. Scudder's research team. He was also studying at Columbia
University to earn an advanced **degree**, a doctorate in medical
science. To earn this degree, a student would study improvements
in the science of medicine.

The newlyweds
shared a New York City
apartment with another
couple and managed to
live on less than $100 a
month. Their budget was
very tight. Lenore joked
that although Drew
always managed to look
neat, his only two suits
were cheap. His shoes
were cracked, but they
were always polished.

Harlem in 1940.

Drew earned a doctorate in medical science in 1940 with his **dissertation**, "Banked Blood: A Study in Blood Preservation." He was the first African American to earn this particular degree.

Charlie and Lenore moved back to Washington, DC, and Charlie returned to his jobs at Howard University and Freedmen's Hospital. Blood storage had become such a large part of the Drews' life that their first daughter, Roberta, was nicknamed "BeBe" (for "blood bank").

The Drew family in 1947

For years Drew had been gathering information and experimenting with the storage of blood. He was determined to find a way to store blood for a longer period of time. The red blood cells were the problem. They determine the different types of blood (A, B, AB, or O). They are also the part of the blood that breaks down after 24 hours and makes the blood unsafe. So Drew had been doing experiments with blood **plasma**, the clear, liquid part of blood.

One day, while working in his lab, Drew asked himself a few important questions: Why use whole blood for transfusions? What would happen if we used only plasma for transfusions? Would that work? Could plasma alone save lives?

Whole blood contains four elements: red blood cells, white blood cells, **platelets**, and plasma. Because plasma doesn't contain red blood cells, it could be given to anybody with any blood type. It could also be stored for a month, frozen for years, and even dried.

Firefighters put out flames in London after the Battle of Britain in 1941.

Drew's research and discoveries couldn't have come at a better time. In 1940, the world desperately needed transfusions to save lives. World War II was raging in Europe, and Germany was bombing England nightly. For 57 straight nights, London was attacked by German airplanes. This ongoing attack was called the "Blitz," short for a German word meaning "lightning war." Thousands of people were killed and injured. England needed blood for transfusions—and fast.

Under Dr. Drew's leadership, by January 1941 the Blood for Britain program had collected more than 14,000 blood donations and safely shipped over 5,000 liters of plasma to England.

Dr. John Beattie, who had been one of Drew's professors at McGill, was in charge of England's blood program, but the supply wasn't big enough to help everyone injured in the "Blitz." The British needed help from the United States. Beattie remembered his brightest student and asked Drew to be the director of the "Blood for Britain" program. He sent a telegram that said, "Could you secure five thousand **ampules** dried plasma for transfusion work immediately and follow this by equal quantity in three or four weeks?"

Drew knew this was impossible, but the impossible had never stopped him before. He wrote back, "There are not five thousand ampules of dried plasma in the world but assistance will be forthcoming."

American Red Cross workers examining plasma in 1941.

Chapter Four

BLOOD BANKS

Charles Drew believed that people must have faith in themselves and go forward with a sure step. In times of emergency, Drew's steps were sure and quick. The question was how to collect such a huge amount of blood in a short amount of time. First, Drew set up blood banks in eight New York City hospitals to collect blood from hundreds of donors who came every day. Soon it became clear that even eight hospitals could not collect the needed amount quickly enough, so he outfitted trucks with refrigerators and nurses and sent these mobile blood banks all over the city.

Dr. Drew with members of the mobile unit of Columbia-Presbyterian Medical Center. They were part of the team that collected blood for the "Blood for Britain" program.

After five months, England set up its own blood banks based on the American models Drew had established. Drew thought he could go finally home to Washington, DC. But the United States would soon be involved in World War II. American soldiers would need the help of Dr. Charles Drew.

American Red Cross poster from the 1940s.

In February of 1941, the Red Cross named Drew the assistant director of the National Blood Collection Program. He opened blood banks all over the United States to collect life-giving blood. When Japan bombed Pearl Harbor on December 7, 1941, the United States had the blood plasma needed to treat the injured. Drew was now working 18-hour days. When Lenore urged him to slow down, he would say, "I'm a sprinter, Lenore, remember." To see more of her husband, Lenore joined him as his lab assistant.

Drew's work with the Red Cross saved the lives of hundreds of thousands of soldiers and **civilians**, both Black and white. Drew couldn't believe it when he learned that the U.S. Armed Forces had issued a policy segregating the blood of white people from the blood of Black people. Because segregation policies ran deep in the United States at that time, the military mistakenly thought that blood should also be segregated, and the Red Cross agreed.

Drew was furious. This was an insult to his race and to his science. He called a press conference to speak with reporters and asked, "How have we, in this age and hour, allowed once again to creep into our hearts the dark myths and wretched superstitions of the past?... Will we ever share a common brotherhood?" Drew went on to explain that there was no scientific reason for separating the blood except on the basis of the four different blood types. Type A blood was type A blood; it wasn't Black or white blood.

Shortly thereafter, Drew resigned from the Red Cross and returned to Howard University. Some people thought Drew had resigned because the Armed Forces refused to change its policy. Lenore set them straight, saying, "I never knew Charles to run from a fight."

These soldiers are donating blood before leaving for duty overseas.

Chapter Five

WE'LL ALL GET THERE TOGETHER

Back at Howard University, Drew continued to do what he believed was his greatest contribution to medicine—training young Black students to become surgeons. His lectures were so popular that when students learned Dr. Drew was making his rounds at the hospital to discuss his cases, they crowded in to hear him. Over and over, he encouraged his students not to accept being second best, but instead to be among the very best.

Drew in 1947.

Drew truly cared about his students, almost as a father would care about his children. When one student showed up in less than spotless clothes one day, Drew offered to do his laundry! That student understood that Dr. Drew wanted him always to look his best, and he never showed up in dirty clothes again.

It was extremely important that Drew's students do well. If they performed poorly, it would be difficult for all African American surgeons to work in white hospitals. He used to tell his class, "We're going to turn out surgeons here who will not have to apologize to anybody, anywhere!"

The day his first students took their American Board of Surgery exams, Drew was so nervous that he went down to the basement with a hammer and beat an old, useless coal bin to pieces. Lenore recalls that the hammering went on for hours—until

Dr. Drew teaching students at Freedmen's Hospital in 1947.

the president of Howard University called to say that "Charlie's Boys" had come in first and second in the exam!

But even with the finest training, many Black doctors could not practice in white hospitals. The American Medical Association (AMA) is the most powerful association for doctors in the United States. Members of the AMA are professional doctors with high standards. At the time, many white hospitals would only hire AMA doctors, but the AMA had never admitted a Black doctor to the association.

This situation made Drew very angry. Black doctors weren't being treated as professionals because they weren't members of the AMA. Black patients couldn't be treated by their Black doctors in white hospitals. Drew wrote to the AMA again and again asking them to end their hundred years of **bigotry**. The AMA did not change its policy on discrimination until 1968, 18 years after Dr. Charles Drew's death.

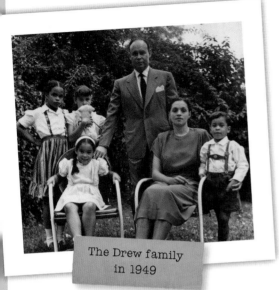

The Drew family in 1949

Sprinting through life left Drew little time to stay home, but that's the place he loved best. He loved playing with his four children. In his free time, Drew enjoyed music. He played the piano, saxophone, and ukulele. He also liked taking photographs, going to the movies, cooking, and gardening at the family's home on the Howard University campus.

Charles Drew's life ended far too soon. March 31, 1950, had been a very busy day. Drew performed several operations, spoke at a student council banquet, took a two-hour nap, kissed his wife goodbye, and headed for Tuskegee, Alabama.

Drew and three other doctors were on their way to a conference in Tuskegee. They planned on driving straight through to Alabama because it was difficult for Black travelers to find hotel rooms at that time. After a coffee break, Drew took his turn driving, but he was exhausted and soon dozed off. The car swerved and went off the road near Burlington, North Carolina, flipping three times. The other doctors weren't seriously hurt, but Drew's chest was crushed, and one of his legs was horribly wounded.

The ambulance arrived and rushed all four doctors to the Alamance General Hospital. The hospital doctors worked to save Drew and gave him blood transfusions, but his injuries were too serious. An hour and a half later, Dr. Charles Richard Drew was dead. It was April 1, 1950, and Drew was only 45 years old.

A rumor arose almost immediately that the white hospital hadn't given Dr. Drew proper medical attention, and that he had bled to death because he was Black. That story wasn't true.

Dr. John R. Ford was one of the doctors in the car when the accident happened. Dr. Ford wrote, "They stopped working immediately on [the less critical] white patients and gave us instant and immediate care. We could not have been treated better. Drew died from a crushing injury, and all the blood in the world could not have saved him."

Dr. Drew's childhood home in Arlington, Virginia, was designated a National Historic Landmark in 1976 by the National Park Service to acknowledge Drew's extraordinary achievements in both medicine and civil rights. On June 3, 1981, the U.S. Postal Service issued the Charles R. Drew stamp as part of the Great Americans Series in his honor.

Thousands came to the Nineteenth Street Baptist Church for Drew's funeral. It was the same church that he and his family had attended when he was a boy singing in the choir.

The president of Howard University spoke at the funeral, saying, "Here we have what rarely happens in history, a life which crowds into a handful of years a significance so great, men will never forget."

How could Charles Richard Drew ever be forgotten? He touched the lives of so many people. His work with plasma and blood transfusions saved countless lives. His work continues today in every blood bank in the world. He inspired a whole generation of Black doctors to overcome the odds, become the very best doctors, and teach others to be the very best as well. Charlie Drew, "the father of the blood bank," never settled for second best. He dedicated his life to the service of others, sprinted his way into history, and forever won a place in the hearts of the American people.

**A person's identity is who they are:
their qualities, what they believe in, etc.**
What part of Drew's identity do you think people noticed first?
What part do you think was most important to him?
What part do you think he struggled most with?

**What does Drew's determination to get into
medical school say about his character?**
Think about your answer.

TIME LINE

1900-1920

1904
Charles Richard Drew
is born on June 3 in
Washington, DC.

1922
Drew graduates from
Dunbar High School.

1926
Drew graduates from
Amherst College in
Massachusetts. He takes
a job at Morgan State
College as the athletic
director and a biology
and chemistry teacher.

1930

1933
Drew graduates as a doctor
of medicine and a master
of surgery from McGill
University in Montreal,
Canada.

1935
Howard University hires
Drew as an instructor and
assistant surgeon. He is also
a resident in surgery at
Freedmen's Hospital.

1936
Drew becomes an instructor
of surgery at Howard
University.

1938
Columbia University
Medical School awards Drew
a fellowship for advanced
training in surgery.

1939
Drew is named director
of Columbia-Presbyterian
Medical Center's blood
bank. He and Minnie
Lenore Robbins marry
on September 23.

As Drew's work with the Red Cross pointed out, blood types have nothing to do with race. He talked about how the very stuff of what the body is made of is the same in all people, no matter their skin color.
If this is true, what is the argument for only giving
white people blood from other white people?

The AMA did not admit a Black doctor until 1968.
What does this say about the quality of the organization's standards?
How do you think the AMA set its standards?
Is every standard that is set right and just?

1940

1950-1960

1940
Drew earns a doctor of science in medicine degree from Columbia University Medical School. He becomes an assistant professor of surgery at Howard University and a surgeon at Freedmen's Hospital. He is also named director of the "Blood for Britain" program.

1941
In February, the Red Cross names Drew the assistant director of the National Blood Collection Program. On December 7, the Japanese bomb Pearl Harbor in

Honolulu, Hawaii, bringing the United States into World War II. Working with the Red Cross blood-banking program, Drew helps ensure that there is enough blood to help soldiers injured in the war.

1949
Drew tours Europe as a surgical consultant to the U.S. Army.

1950
Drew dies in an automobile accident near Burlington, North Carolina, on April 1.

1952
The Washington, DC chapter of the American Medical Association (AMA) agrees to accept Black members.

1968
The AMA ends its policy of racial discrimination, 18 years after Drew's death.

ampules (AM-pyoolz)
Ampules are very small glass jars used to hold a liquid. Dr. Beattie asked Dr. Drew to find 5,000 ampules of dried plasma for British war victims.

bigotry (BIG-uh-tree)
Bigotry is a strong dislike for people of a certain group, such as those of a different race or religion. Drew asked the American Medical Association to end its 100 years of bigotry against African Americans.

certified (SUR-tih-fyd)
If something is certified, it has been officially approved. Canada certified Drew as a surgical specialist.

civilians (sih-VIL-yunz)
Civilians are people who are not part of the armed forces. Drew's work with the Red Cross saved the lives of civilians as well as soldiers.

dean (DEEN)
A dean is the head of a college or school at a university. At Amherst, a dean urged Drew to decide whether sports or education was more important to him.

degree (deh-GREE)
In education, a degree is a title given to a student who graduates from a college or university program. Drew earned several degrees related to medicine.

dissertation (diss-ser-TAY-shun)
A dissertation is a long paper that a student writes to earn an advanced degree. To earn his doctor of science in medicine degree, Drew wrote a dissertation called "Banked Blood: A Study in Blood Preservation."

fellowship (FELL-oh-ship)
A fellowship is a paid position given to someone at a school or other organization, often in honor of his or her achievements. Drew was awarded a fellowship to Columbia University Medical School in New York City.

influenced (IN-floo-enst)
To be influenced by something is to be strongly affected by it. The Reverend Walter Brooks influenced Drew's ideas about what to do with his life.

plasma (PLAZ-muh)
Plasma is the clear liquid in which blood cells float. Drew made great progress in working with blood plasma.

platelets (PLAYT-letz)
Platelets are tiny, flat particles in blood. The platelets are one of four elements that make up whole blood.

racial (RAY-shul)
Racial means having to do with a person's race. Drew's first daily experiences with racial hatred and slurs happened at Amherst College.

scholarship (SKAHL-er-ship)
A scholarship is money awarded to a student to help pay for his or her education. Amherst College in Massachusetts gave Drew a partial scholarship.

segregated (SEG-reh-gay-ted)
If people or things are segregated, they are kept apart. Many places in the United States were once segregated, so African Americans either could not enter or were kept separate from white people.

transfusion (trans-FYOO-zhun)
A transfusion is the transfer of blood from one person to another. Thousands of people needed transfusions during World War II.

tuberculosis (tuh-bur-kyuh-LOH-sis)
Tuberculosis is a disease that attacks people's lungs. Dr. Drew's sister died of tuberculosis.

BOOKS

Adamson, Thomas K. *World War II*. Mankato, MN: The Child's World 2015.

DK. *World War II: Visual Encyclopedia*. New York, NY: DK Publishing, 2015.

Schraff, Anne E. *The Life of Dr. Charles Drew: Blood Bank Innovator*. Berkeley Heights, NJ: Enslow Publishers, 2015.

Showers, Paul. *A Drop of Blood*. New York, NY: HarperCollins, 2004.

Venezia, Mike. *Charles Drew*. New York, NY: Scholastic, 2009.

WEBSITES

Visit our website for links about Dr. Charles Drew:

childsworld.com/links

Note to Parents, Teachers, and Librarians: We routinely verify our Web links to make sure they are safe, active sites—so encourage your readers to check them out!

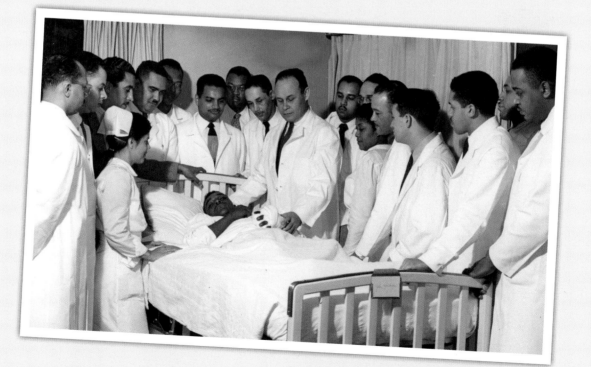